● soho
● theatre company

Soho Theatre Company presents

T0347804

MERCY

by **Lin Coghlan**

First performed at Soho Theatre on 8 July 2004

Performances in the Lorenz Auditorium

Soho Theatre is supported by

Registered Charity No: 267234

Soho Theatre Company productions are supported by the Garfield Weston Foundation.

Soho Theatre Company presents

MERCY

By **Lin Coghlan**

Cookie	Danny Worters
Deccy	Andrew Garfield
Jean	Samantha King
Mac	Adam Rhys Dee
Rory	Peter Sullivan
Terry	Elliott Jordan

Directed by	Paul Miller
Designed by	Hayden Griffin
Lighting by	Andy Phillips
Sound by	John Leonard
Costume by	Chris Chahill
Casting	Ginny Schiller

Production Manager	Nick Ferguson
Stage Manager	Dani Youngman
Deputy Stage Manager	Tamara Albachari
Assistant Stage Manager	Sally Higson
Chief Technician	Nick Blount
Chief Electrician	Christoph Wagner
Lighting Technician	Ade Peterkin
Scenery built and painted by	Robert Knight Ltd

Press Representation	Nancy Poole (020 7478 0142)
Photography	Adrian Neal / Getty Images

Soho Theatre and Writers' Centre
21 Dean Street
London W1D 3NE
Admin: 020 7287 5060
Fax: 020 7287 5061
Box Office: 0870 429 6883
www.sohotheatre.com
email: box@sohotheatre.com

Cast

Andrew Garfield Deccy

Andrew trained at the Central School of Speech and Drama. Credits whilst at Drama School include *Hamlet*, *A Midsummer Night's Dream*, *Absolute Hell*, *The Kitchen*, *Troilus and Cressida*, *The Country Wife*, *All My Sons* and *Philistines*.

Elliott Jordan Terry

Elliott trained at the Sylvia Young Theatre School. Theatre credits include *Beautiful Thing* (Nottingham Playhouse/National Tour) and *The Adventures of Nicholas Nickleby* (National Youth Theatre). Television credits include *Murphy's Law*, *Murder*, *Double Take* (Tiger Aspect); *Reps* (Tyne Tees TV); *Lock Stock* (SKA Ginger Productions) and *London's Burning* (LWT). Film credits include *New Town Original* (New Town Films); *The Toybox* (Brandnew Films) and *Fogbound* (Mulholland Pictures).

Samantha King Jean

Samantha King trained at the Italia Conti Academy of Theatre Arts. Recent credits include *Harry Potter and the Philosopher's Stone* (Warner Brothers); *The Bill* (ITV); *Urban Rites* (LWT) and *The Hoobs* (Channel 4). Samantha has also performed various radio plays for Radio 4.

Adam Rhys Dee Mac

Adam trained at the National Youth Theatre and at the Arts Educational School, London. Theatre credits include *Funny About Love* (Mill at Sonning Theatre). Television credits include *Gods and Godesses* and *Doctors* (BBC).

Peter Sullivan Rory

Peter's theatre credits include *Revelations* (Gateway Theatre, Chester); *Our Town, Action Replay, Measure for Measure* (Contact Theatre, Manchester); *La Fura Dels Baus Company* (World Tour); *The Bacchae* (Opera Factory); *The Runners, Musicians, Alien Activity, Napoli Milionaria, Richard III, King Lear* (National Theatre); *The Way of the World* (Lyric, Hammersmith); *Certain Young Men, Lulu* (Almeida) and *Drummers* (New Ambassadors Theatre).

Danny Worters Cookie

Danny's theatre credits include *Les Liaisons Dangereuses* (P & S Productions); *Sliding with Suzanne* (Royal Court); *Conversations with my Father* (Old Vic); *The Cryptogram* (Ambassadors Theatre); *The Life of Galileo* (Almeida) and *The Gingerbread House* (Watermans Arts Centre). Television credits include *Holby City, All the King's Men, The Broker's Man, Children of the New Forest, Henry IV parts I and II, Sorry About Last Night, Knowing Me, Knowing You* (BBC); *Bliss* (ITV) and *Kiss and Tell* (LWT).

Company

Lin Coghlan Writer

Lin is from Dublin. She trained at The Rose Bruford College and for ten years wrote almost exclusively for non-traditional theatre venues in schools, factories, prisons, drop-in centres and homeless projects with companies which included Theatre Centre (who commissioned her to write her first play), Red Ladder, the Irish Company, Nottingham Roundabout, and the Half Moon Young People's Theatre. Plays include *Waking* (Soho Theatre); *Bretevski Street*, *A Feeling in My Bones* (Theatre Centre); *The Night Garden* (National Theatre Studio/Northcott Theatre Exeter); *With Love from Nicolae* (Teatrul Dramatic Constanza/Bristol Old Vic); *Apache Tears* (Clean Break – joint winner of The Peggy Ramsay Award); *Rising Blue* (RNT Studio – Translation) and *Mercy* (finalist for the Susan Smith Blackburn Award). Film credits include *Electric Frank* (BBC Films, winner of the Special Prize – Locarno and Toronto Film Festivals) and *First Communion Day* (BBC Films, winner of the Dennis Potter Play of the Year Award). Radio credits include *Passing*, *2,000 Tales*, *Les Miserables* (adaptation) and *Mansfield Park* (adaptation) for BBC Radio 4. Lin is currently writing a new play for The Bush, she has a full length feature film in development and her television series *Intergalactic Patrick* (BBC) is shooting this summer.

Chris Chahill Costume Designer

Christopher studied set/costume design at Croydon School of Art. His design credits for theatre include *Our Country's Good* (Nuffield Theatre, Southampton); *Essential Remains* (Copley Theatre, Boston); *An English Man Abroad* (Bridewell Theatre); *Time, Tempo, Tune* (Peacock Theatre); *Musicals around the World* (Das Festspiel Haus,Vienna); *Edward II* (Kings Head); *Independent State* (Sydney Opera House) and *First Years and Beginnings* (Latchmere Theatre). As Associate Designer/Supervisor his credits include *Sing Yer Heart Out for the Lads* (National Theatre); *Honeymoon Suite* (Royal Court); *Taking Sides* (UK Tour) and *Auntie and Me* (Wyndhams Theatre).

Hayden Griffin Designer

Hayden Griffin's theatre work spans 30 years and includes 36 World Premier productions with writers and directors such as David Hare (including *Plenty*, *A Map of the World* and *Pravda*), David Mamet (*Glengarry Glen Ross*), Edward Bond (including *Summer*), Howard Brenton, William Gaskill and Bill Bryden for the National Theatre, the RSC, Royal Court and many West End theatres. Hayden has designed opera and ballet for major world centres including the Royal Opera House, ENO and Birmingham Royal Ballet, collaborating with David Bintley (including *Still Life at the Penguin Café*), Guilini and Bernard Haitink (*Parsifal*). Hayden's most recent credit is *Sing Yer Heart Out for the Lads* at the National Theatre.

John Leonard Sound Designer

John started work in theatre sound 30 years ago and during that time he has provided soundtracks for theatres all over the world. Recent productions for Soho Theatre include *Flush, Wrong Place, A Reckoning, Things You Shouldn't Say Past Midnight, Meeting Myself Coming Back* and *Kiss Me Like You Mean It*. Other recent productions include *The Dumb Waiter* (Oxford Playhouse); *Still Life/The Astonished Heart* – Double Bill, *The Entertainer* (Liverpool Everyman and Playhouse); *Les Liaisons Dangereuses* (West End); *Sweet Panic* (West End); *Absolutely! (perhaps)* (West End); *Jumpers* (National Theatre/West End); *The Master Builder* (Tour and West End); *Private Lives* (West End/Broadway); *Midnight's Children* (London, Tour and USA), *Antony and Cleopatra* (RSC); *The Merry Wives of Windsor* (Ludlow Festival); *Sunday Father* (Hampstead Theatre); *Madame Tussaud's Exhibition* (New York/Amsterdam) and *Five Gold Rings, The Mercy Seat, I.D., The Lady From The Sea* (Almeida Theatre). John is a director of Aura Sound Design Ltd.

Paul Miller Director

Paul's theatre credits include *Sing Yer Heart Out for the Lads* (National Theatre); *Honeymoon Suite* (English Touring Theatre/Royal Court); *Fragile Land* (Hampstead Theatre); *The Associate* (National Theatre/Tour); *Mean Tears* (Sheffield Crucible); *Four Nights in Knaresborough* (National Tour); *Tragedy: a tragedy* (Gate); *Accomplices, Mr England* (National Theatre/ Sheffield Crucible); *A Penny for a Song* (Oxford Stage Co/Whitehall); *Hushabye Mountain* (ETT/Hampstead Theatre); *Rosmersholm* (Southwark Playhouse); *The Robbers* (Latchmere); *Sugar Sugar, Goldhawk Road, Bad Company* (Bush Theatre) and extensive work at the National Theatre Studio. Opera credits include *The Marriage of Figaro* (ETO). Radio credits include *Unsinkable* (Radio 3).

Andy Phillips Lighting Designer

Andy Phillips' career began at the Royal Court in 1965. Since then he has worked all over the world. At the National, productions include *A Woman Killed with Kindness, The Misanthrope, Equus, The Iceman Cometh, Golden Boy, Glengarry Glen Ross, Galileo, The Mountain Giants, Cardiff East* and *Sing Yer Heart Out for the Lads*. At the RSC, *New England, A Patriot For Me, Son of Man* and *In the Company of Men*. Most recently in the West End, *Auntie and Me* and, at the Royal Court, *Honeymoon Suite*. He has received two Tony nominations, for *Equus* and *M Butterfly*.

● **soho**
● theatre company

Soho Theatre Company is passionate in its commitment to new writing, producing a year-round programme of bold, original and accessible new plays – many of them from first-time playwrights.

'a foundry for new talent... one of the country's leading producers of new writing' Evening Standard

Soho Theatre + Writers' Centre offers an invaluable resource to emerging playwrights. Our training and outreach programme includes the innovative Under 11's scheme, the Young Writers' Group (15-25s) and a burgeoning series of Nuts and Bolts writing workshops designed to equip new writers with the basic tools of playwriting. We offer the nation's only unsolicited script-reading service, reporting on over 2,000 plays per year. We aim to develop and showcase the most promising new work through the national Verity Bargate Award, the Launch Pad scheme and the Writers' Attachment Programme, working to develop writers not just in theatre but also for TV and film.

'a creative hotbed... not only the making of theatre but the cradle for new screenplay and television scripts' The Times

Contemporary, comfortable, air-conditioned and accessible, Soho Theatre is busy from early morning to late at night. Alongside the production of new plays, it is also an intimate venue to see leading national and international comedians in an eclectic programme mixing emerging new talent with established names.

'London's coolest theatre by a mile' Midweek

Soho Theatre Company is developing its work outside the building, producing in Edinburgh and on tour in the UK whilst expanding the scope of its work with writers. It hosts the annual Soho Writers' Festival which brings together innovative practitioners from the creative industries with writers working in theatre, film, TV, radio, literature and poetry. Our programme aims to challenge, entertain and inspire writers and audiences from all backgrounds.

Soho Theatre and Writers' Centre
Soho Theatre + Writers' Centre
21 Dean Street
London W1D 3NE
Admin: 020 7287 5060
Box Office: 0870 429 6883
Minicom: 020 7478 0136
www.sohotheatre.com email: box@sohotheatre.com

● soho
● theatre company

Bars and Restaurant

Café Lazeez brasserie serves Indian-fusion dishes until 12pm. Late bar open until 1am. The Terrace Bar serves a range of soft and alcoholic drinks.

Email information list

For regular programme updates and offers, join our free email information list by emailing box@sohotheatre.com or visiting www.sohotheatre.com/mailing.
If you would like to make any comments about any of the productions seen at Soho Theatre, visit our chatroom at www.sohotheatre.com

Hiring the theatre

Soho Theatre has a range of rooms and spaces for hire. Please contact the theatre managers on 020 7287 5060, email hires@sohotheatre.com or go to www.sohotheatre.com for further details.

● soho
● theatre company

Artistic Director: Abigail Morris
Acting Artistic Director: Jonathan Lloyd
Assistant to Artistic Director: Nadine Hoare
Administrative Producer: Mark Godfrey
Assistant to Administrative Producer: Tim Whitehead
Writers' Centre Director: Nina Steiger
Literary Officer: David Lane
Education and Workshop Officer: Suzanne Gorman
Casting Director: Ginny Schiller
Marketing and Development Director: Zoe Reed
Development Manager: Gayle Rogers
Marketing Officer: Jenni Wardle
Marketing and Development Assistant: Kelly Duffy
Press Officer: Nancy Poole (020 7478 0142)
General Manager: Catherine Thornborrow
Front of House and Building Manager: Julia Christie
Financial Controller: Kevin Dunn
Book Keeper: Elva Tehan
Box Office Manager: Kate Truefitt
Deputy Box Office Manager: Steve Lock
Box Office Assistants: Janice Draper, Jennie Fellows, Richard Gay, Paula Henstock, Leah Read, Will Sherriff Hammond and Natalie Worrall.
Duty Managers: Mike Owen, Rebecca Storey, Peter Youthed and Miranda Yates
Front of House staff: Rachel Bavidge, Louise Beere, Sharon Degan, Matthew Halpin, Tom Holloway, Siobhan Hyams, Colin Goodwin, Katherine Smith, Rachel Southern, Maya Symeou, Luke Tebbutt, Minho Kwon and Jamie Zubairi

Production Manager: Nick Ferguson
Chief Technician: Nick Blount
Chief LX: Christoph Wagner
Lighting Technician: Ade Peterkin

THE SOHO THEATRE DEVELOPMENT CAMPAIGN

Soho Theatre Company receives core funding from Arts Council England, London and Westminster City Council. In order to provide as diverse a programme as possible and expand our audience development and outreach work, we rely upon additional support from trusts, foundations, individuals and businesses.

All of our major sponsors share a common commitment to developing new areas of activity and encouraging creative partnerships between business and the arts.

We are immensely grateful for the invaluable support from our sponsors and donors and wish to thank them for their continued commitment.

Soho Theatre Company has launched a new Friends Scheme to support its work in developing new writers and reaching new audiences. To find out how to become a Friend of Soho Theatre and what you will receive in return, contact the development department on 020 7478 0111, email development@sohotheatre.com or visit www.sohotheatre.com

Sponsors: Angels Costumiers, Arts & Business, Bloomberg, Getty Images, TBWA\GGT

Major Supporters: Calouste Gulbenkian Foundation · The Foyle Foundation · The Paul Hamlyn Foundation · Roger and Cecil Jospé · John Lyon's Charity · The Wellcome Trust · The Garfield Weston Foundation · The Harold Hyam Wingate Foundation · Roger Wingate

Education Patrons: Tony and Rita Gallagher · Nigel Gee · Jack and Linda Keenan

Trusts and Foundations: Anon · Sidney and Elizabeth Corob Charitable Trust · Delfont Foundation · The Follett Trust · JG Hogg Charitable Trust · Hyde Park Place Estate Charity · John Lewis, Oxford Street · Linbury Trust · The Mackintosh Foundation · The Moose Foundation for the Arts · The Royal Victoria Hall Foundation · The St James's Trust · The Kobler Trust · Tesco Charity Trust · The Hazel Wood Charitable Trust

Dear Friends: Anonymous · Jill and Michael Barrington · Madeleine Hamel · Robert Paddick, Commonwealth Partners Ltd. · SoFie and Le'le' · Richard and Diana Toeman · Jan and Michael Topham

Friends: Thank you also to the many Soho Friends we are unable to list here. For a full list of our patrons, please visit www.sohotheatre.com

Registered Charity: 267234

Introduction

For eight years I lived on a council estate in South London not unlike the one where Mac and Cookie grew up. There was 80% unemployment, a serious drug problem, daily assaults, hundreds of families struggling to cope on benefits which were repeatedly paid late, or incorrectly – it was a moneylenders' paradise. It was also a source of great stories: the tenant who filled his whole flat up with earth – the bloke who spent weeks demolishing his flat with a sledge hammer in some sort of protest – the villain who did over the dry cleaners with a shotgun only to be traced straight back to his flat because he was one of the shop's best customers and they had his name and address from the last time they pressed his trousers. There were tragedies too – staggering rates of mental illness, scores of young men suffering with schizophrenia – one in particular who spent all his waking hours in the car park staring at the sky as if awaiting rescue from outer space. Into this war zone, every day, babies were born. By five years old they were hardened operators. They knew everything from how to blag a bag of chips to where the best place was to ditch a firearm. Of course there were exceptions – plenty of them – kids whose parents kept it together somehow – girls who had the support of a canny Aunt or Gran – families who did well – who were the second generation to grow up in those blocks since the war – who worked 80-hour weeks in three different jobs so their kids might have a better chance then they had.

More recently I've worked as a writer in prisons, both here in England and abroad. I began to see the faces of those undernourished kids again in the young men and women who found themselves confined and on the wrong side of the law.

Yet, amongst these offenders, often in the most unlikely individuals, I repeatedly came across the unmistakable presence of compassion. The skinhead who had lost his privileges for fighting – who was inside for a string of violent crimes, yet who tenderly cared for his rescued pigeon; the older man, in and out of prison all his life, who wept when he talked about his beloved childhood dog. Here were men I recognised – men who were catapulted from babydom to the adult world in one juddering step. I wanted to write their stories, not as an apology, or as some sort of explanation, but rather to record simply what I had seen. I became aware in the process that a pattern was emerging in the experiences of many of the incarcerated men and women with whom I worked – behind each of their stories often lay the remnants of a childhood in ruins, for which I cannot help but feel we all bear some responsibility.

Lin Coghlan
London 2004

Thanks

I would like to thank Jack Bradley and Sue Higginson at The Royal National Theatre Studio without whom this play would never have been written; Paul Miller for his invaluable insight, advice and encouragement, and finally Joan Scanlon for reading the text, and for her support.

MERCY

This play is dedicated to Nancy Diuguid
with love and respect

First published in 2004 by Oberon Books Ltd
(incorporating Absolute Classics)
521 Caledonian Road, London N7 9RH
Tel: 020 7607 3637 / Fax: 020 7607 3629
e-mail: oberon.books@btinternet.com
www.oberonbooks.com

A catalogue record for this book is available from the British
Library.

ISBN: 1 84002 451 8

Characters

COOKIE

MAC

DECCY

TERRY

JEAN

RORY

There is a non-speaking female role, STELLA,
who may or may not appear on stage, at the
production's discretion.

Scene One

Wind.

Rain.

COOKIE stands in the mud looking at us.

COOKIE: It was so fucking dark – that's cause it was the countryside Mac said. You couldn't see nothing, not straight off anyhow. We had a look in the car first, she had all sorts in the back.

MAC: Fucking laptop. Intel Pentium.

DECCY: You wanker.

MAC: What?

COOKIE: Then Deccy says…

DECCY: Come on Mac. It aint nothing to do with us is it?

COOKIE: It was that dark, and when the rain come down, you couldn't hardly hear your own voice, like it was took right out of your head. Everyone sounded different that night. Changed.

MAC comes through the muddy grass shivering in a T-shirt and jeans. He's been smacked about. DECCY follows him.

DECCY: I think they've gone man.

MAC: Fuckers.

DECCY: No Mac, I think they've fucking gone.

MAC: Took our fucking mobiles, bastards.

DECCY: (*Looks around scared.*) Think Cookie's alright?

MAC looks out over the land.

I told you man.

MAC rubs his arms to keep warm.

MAC: You fucking made sure they got to know about us.

DECCY: Mac, man…

MAC: You fucking did. Gobbing off in front of Terry
     Bennet down Peters Street…

DECCY: I didn't.

MAC: You can't be trusted.

DECCY: I fucking can Mac.

They look at each other.

I fucking can be trusted.

Beat.

Fucks sake.

MAC: You got any money?

DECCY: I aint got nothing. They took it, didn't they?

They look around in the cold dark night.

MAC: Where the fuck are we man?

DECCY: (*Looking around.*) Some field. Can't even see the
     fucking edges.

MAC: Can't go back. Fucks sake. We can't go back never
     man. They'll kill us if we go back.

They rub their arms trying to keep warm.

DECCY: Don't matter. Probably never even find our way
     out of this fucking field.

*Nearby. COOKIE stands wet and lost in a field. He's a
fifteen year old boy with learning difficulties.*

COOKIE: Mac? Mac? I dropped the bag, I didn't mean to.

COOKIE waits.

COOKIE: Mac. We got to go home. We got to go home Mac.

Back with MAC and DECCY.

MAC: We just got to wait here don't we? They aint gonna stay out here all night. Fucks sake, they'll want to get off home sooner or later.

DECCY: They said they was gonna get us.

MAC: Well they got us, didn't they? .

DECCY: Yeah.

Beat.

DECCY: You think that's what they meant?

MAC: What else could they mean?

DECCY: (*Shouting.*) Cookie!

MAC: Shut the fuck up will you? They'll hear you.

DECCY: You said they'd have gone home.

MAC: Let's just wait and see, eh?

Back with COOKIE.

COOKIE: When I saw her I couldn't see nothing much at first like. And I'm thinking, fucks sake, it might be those lads. But it didn't sound like them. First of all I seen something shining like, turns out to be her eyes. She's just hanging there in this hedge. This woman just hanging in this hedge.

MAC: You got a smoke?

DECCY: Yeah.

DECCY makes a roll up, they both look around nervously.

DECCY: Is that lights – over there?

MAC: (*Straining to see.*) Dunno.

DECCY: It aint a car is it?

MAC: Aint moving.

DECCY: That fucking Ford.

MAC: Fucking shit car. Wankers.

DECCY: Banged me head in the boot.

DECCY rubs his head. Hands MAC the roll up. They smoke.

MAC: One of them was that Slater's brother. The one that done time in Brixton.

DECCY: Which one?

MAC: The one with the steel toe caps. Clubbed that fat bloke down the Regent.

DECCY: You think Cookie's waiting for us?

MAC: Looked like him anyhow. Wanker.

DECCY: They shouldn't have took Cookie. I mean, fucks sake man, what's it got to do with Cookie?

MAC: He's my brother.

COOKIE: It's that dark and I can hear this gurgling sound. Turns out to be this woman – breathing. Gurgling like water going down a plughole. Thought it could be them blokes off the estate but it don't sound like them. Why you there in that hedge like that? I look around, can't see nothing. You having me on or what?

COOKIE moves closer.

Fucks sake, you...fucks sake, you got this...wooden thing, right through you.

DECCY: We could die of exposure out here.

MAC: In April?

DECCY: It's still fucking cold.

MAC: We don't have to go home Deccy.

DECCY: Where we gonna go then?

MAC: They'd think we was dead or something. If we never went back.

DECCY: What about me mum?

MAC: You hate your fucking mum.

They gaze out over the dark night.

We could just walk away. Never see that fucking estate again. Get new names – identities.

DECCY: What's my name then? Me new identity?

MAC: Eddie. Eddie Michaels

DECCY: Eddie?

MAC: You got a big family down Dagenham but your dad's a right wanker.

DECCY: I aint got a dad.

MAC: Eddie Michaels has.

DECCY: What's your name then?

MAC: Demitreo Stephanos.

DECCY: Fucks sake.

MAC: Greek.

DECCY: You wanker.

MAC: Alright Eddie?

DECCY: Yeah. Alright…

MAC: Demitreo.

DECCY: You wanker.

MAC: Just walk away. Say fuck you and walk.

DECCY: What's that?

MAC: What?

DECCY: Over there.

Both the boys look – scared.

It's a light.

COOKIE climbs over the hedge a torch in his hand.

COOKIE: Found your motor. It's a right mess. I like this torch, it's big, isn't it?

Silence.

(*Shining his torch at the sky.*) You seen them stars?

COOKIE stands shining his torch up into the sky.

They're that far away.

COOKIE shines his torch into the night sky.

You want a drink? I got a Tango.

COOKIE pulls the ring on the can of drink. He gives a drink to STELLA.

I saw this bloke on the telly got an iron spike through his head and he didn't feel nothing.

Beat.

My brother's going to be here soon. He'll know what to do. I'm not allowed to make big decisions. We got to wait for Mac.

In another part of the muddy field, TERRY and JEAN stand,
two teenagers. He's wearing his Army Cadet uniform.

TERRY: I bought me own gas mask. Then I got one for me
mum, me sister and the dog.

JEAN: Fucks sake Tes, what's your dog gonna look like in a
gas mask? Whole city's going down under chemical
warfare and you've got a fucking gas mask for the dog.

TERRY: Course in a real national disaster it's the panic kills
people. You got to be prepared to defend yourself if a
civilian tries to get your gas mask. Cause someone has
to be in charge don't they? In a national disaster us army
cadets would be called upon to do vital duties in civil
defence and stopping people looting.

JEAN: You'd be the one fucking looting.

TRERRY: No I'd never.

JEAN: We all would.

TERRY: What's the point in looting if there's a national
fucking disaster?

JEAN: But we aint all gonna die are we? And when the
whole of London is like fucking flattened I still want a
wide screen DVD don't I? I mean, fucks sake, we'll still
need the telly.

They look out across the landscape.

TERRY: There's nothing here.

JEAN: I thought it was here.

TERRY: Let's go Jeans.

JEAN: No Tes. I saw something.

TERRY: They'll be looking for us by now.

JEAN: No they won't. Probably aint even noticed I've gone. What you staring at?

TERRY: Nothing. Just…you look nice.

JEAN: Never thought you'd come.

TERRY: Had to wait like didn't I – strategy.

JEAN: You should have seen that Sonia's face. There's this bloke climbing in the window with a big fucking rope.

TERRY: Did it down Army Cadets, didn't we? Going up walls.

JEAN: Glad to see all them skills aint been wasted.

TERRY: Said I'd come for you.

JEAN: Yeah. Just never have anyone do what they promised before – have I?

RORY, a man of thirty five, is sitting on a crate, muddy and dishevelled.

RORY: It's nine twenty and I'm on my way to work – on the tube – trying to get out of my head. I don't want to be here. I'm thinking about when I was seventeen I got this job, working in a recording studio in the Kings Road and I was happy. Thing about happiness is that you don't know you're happy, really happy, till after. But looking back on it now, I remember those days and I think, I was really fucking – contented.

JEAN: Shit. That field we come through. Shit Tes – it's full of water.

They look.

TERRY: It aint even been raining.

JEAN: Was earlier.

TERRY: Fucking hell – what is this?

COOKIE: You want another drink?

COOKIE gives the injured woman another drink. It starts to rain.

Aint you got a coat?

RORY: So anyhow, I can't remember when I first met the little bastard...

MAC: What you looking at?

RORY: Right cocky little toe rag. You Mac then?

MAC: Might be.

RORY: Had that skin they all have. Parched. That white oily skin that's been built up over the years on a diet of chips and coke. You got anything for me?

MAC: You serious?

RORY: Turns out he's got anything you like.

MAC: Fifty to you mate, alright?

RORY: A week later his mum brings him into the office – turns out I'm his new case worker. That was six months ago.

COOKIE: (*Calling.*) She's down here.

COOKIE leads the way with his torch.

MAC: You are so full of shit Cooks.

MAC and DECCY climb over the hedge.

MAC / DECCY: Fucks sake...

MAC: Fucks sake man, she's got...what *is* that?

COOKIE: It's one of them things from the fence.

MAC: It's gone right through her.

DECCY: I feel weird Mac. I'm gonna chuck up, I know I am.

MAC: You sure she aint dead?

DECCY: We got to get out of here.

MAC: Dec's right.

DECCY: We're getting new identities, aint we Mac?

MAC: Come on Cooks.

COOKIE: We can't leave her.

MAC: You what?

COOKIE looks at them.

Course we can. It aint nothing to do with us.

DECCY: Come on Cooks, we got to go.

MAC: Listen Cookie, mate, she's finished, aint she? Look at her.

COOKIE: We could rescue her.

MAC: She's got a fucking great pole through her chest – she aint going nowhere man.

RORY: So, tonight, I go home, really fucking knackered and Rachel says...You got case notes all over the floor Rory. You're not exactly Miss Tidypants yourself Rachel, you know what I mean? Got any wine? Then she says... I'm serious. These are...people's lives.

Beat.

Beer than? She looks at me. I can hear the rain falling against the glass of the kitchen windows. It makes me think about my mum, back home, listening to the radio on that greasy little window sill as she washed up. Never mind eh, got to have something left over from Christmas, here we go. End of the port... Cheers. And she's looking at me – for the last time. We both know it, inevitable, like a storm you can see coming in over the water, and you're just waiting for it to come. Urging it on.

DECCY comes back over the hedge.

DECCY: She's got a fucking laptop in the car man and a personal organiser, fucking CD player.

MAC goes through STELLA's bag.

MAC: Fucking seveny-five quid... Fucks sake. What else she got back there?

MAC goes back over the hedge. DECCY and COOKIE try to keep warm.

DECCY: Don't worry about it Cooks. She'll be dead soon. Me dad used to spike fish down the canal like that. Fucking killed them in no time. Stands to reason.

MAC comes back.

MAC: Dec! Dec! She's only got a brand new Play Station.

DECCY: Fucks sake.

DECCY looks over MAC's shoulder.

Mac? Mac...what's that?

MAC: What's what mate?

DECCY: What *is* that?

MAC, DECCY and COOKIE look.

Is that...water?

RORY: I'm drunk when I leave the Three Brewers at chucking out time, but not drunk enough if you know what I mean. I'm going to leave my job, leave Rachel if she hasn't already left me, leave the fucking flat, leave the country. But I need another drink first so I go up the Laurels. There's an offy with a steel grille over the door: you've got to pass your money through a little gap at the bottom in case you go ape shit, try to get your hands on that bottle of Jamesons, kick the door down and slaughter every member of the West Indian family who stand in their night clothes between you and that drink. The mother serves me in a candlewick dressing gown and fluffy slippers. She hands the bottle out to me through the hatch like a priest giving holy fucking communion.

DECCY: It is. It's fucking – shit man – it's water. Where's it coming from?

MAC: How the fuck should I know? Let's get out of here eh?

COOKIE: What about her?

DECCY: I can't swim Mac.

MAC: You knobhead! You aint gonna have to swim.

COOKIE: We can't just…leave her.

MAC: You are kidding me. Come on mate, I mean – who the fuck is she, we don't even know her, do we?

COOKIE: But we can't leave her.

MAC: She aint nothing to do with us man.

TERRY: It's started, aint it?

JEAN: What has?

TERRY: Fucks sake – the war.

JEAN: Cause there's a flood? You serious?

TERRY: Listen Jeans, they said it could start like this. Look like just normal weather conditions. They do it like that to confuse us. We got to get back.

DECCY: Those lights.

MAC: What?

DECCY: Way over there, like…in a mist.

MAC: Looks like…

DECCY: Fire?

MAC: Cities glow man.

DECCY: Do they?

COOKIE: It wasn't glowing before.

TERRY: You should see my dad Jeans. Fucking bald bastard. My dad goes into fucking Argos Christmas, we aint never seen him since Easter, and he goes down Argos and says 'Give me the Barbie fucking horse set'. That's what he says. 'Give me the Barbie fucking horse set.' So the woman in Argos says, 'You can't talk to me like that, there's kids in here' but my dad couldn't give a toss could he, cause all he wants is to go down Metal Mickeys and get out of his head, so he says 'Give us the Barbie fucking horse set' and the woman presses the alarm, my dad jumps over the counter, grabs this stuffed dog and says – 'I'll have this then instead you stuck up cow,' and he leaves. Christmas day he gives Sandra the dog and she says – 'I asked you for Barbie's Pony' and dad says – he's a bit pissed already – and he turns to her and says – 'Barbie's Pony broke his leg and Ken had to fucking shoot him.'

JEAN laughs and laughs. Finally TERRY starts to laugh too.

TERRY: (*Laughing.*) Fucking bastard.

JEAN: I hate Barbie I do.

TERRY: You aint normal.

Beat.

You know what I hate most about my dad Jeans… his
shoes. He aint got no self respect, you know what I
mean? When I get into the real army I'm going to look
so fucking good.

JEAN: Look good already.

TERRY: Fancy me do you?

JEAN: I was just saying…

TERRY: Cause I fancy you…

He moves towards her.

Come on Jeanie…

JEAN: I thought there was a war starting.

COOKIE: If you leave her here it'll be like what Gran did
to Ginger.

MAC: Fucks sake Cookie.

COOKIE: When we was up Peters Street, before the
Laurels…

MAC: We got to go Cooks…

COOKIE: Dad gets given this ferret in a pub and I call it…

MAC: Fucking Ginger!

DECCY: No man!

MAC: Calls his ferret fucking Ginger…

COOKIE: Mum says I can keep it in a special box on the balcony, but it cries all night...

MAC: Squeals like a fucking rat or something...

COOKIE: And it does its business in my bed sometimes...

MAC: You mean shits man...

DECCY: Gross...

COOKIE: So one day I come home from school and I look everywhere for Ginger...

MAC: Calling all over the fucking flat – Ginger! Ginger!

DECCY's pissing himself.

COOKIE: And Gran says... I got rid of it – dirty thing.

MAC: Chucked it down the rubbish shoot.

COOKIE: Poor Ginger. Poor boy.

MAC: Fucking cruel bitch.

They all look at STELLA.

MAC: We'd never be able to get her off that thing, would we? We'd kill her Cooks.

DECCY: No, you got to leave it in her man. Honest Mac, I saw this programme on the telly...

COOKIE: About the man with the spike in his head?

DECCY: Yeah man. This bloke got this railing right through his head and the firemen, they had to cut it off the fence like and take him to hospital with the thing still in him. Stops the bleeding. Worse thing you can do is pull it out.

MAC: (*Staring, shuddering.*) I wasn't gonna pull it out.

They all look.

DECCY: Got to cut the long bit off though.

MAC: How we gonna do that?

COOKIE: There's a saw in the car.

MAC and DECCY stare at COOKIE.

MAC: Wait a minute – fucks sake. Why are we doing this exactly?

DECCY: Reward man. She'll have money – won't she? We'll be like heroes.

COOKIE: There's loads of water in that ditch Mac. If we don't move her, she'll drown.

MAC: We'll fucking kill her Dec. Send us down for fucking killing her.

DECCY: It's wet, cold, we aint got no phone – she's dead no matter what we do.

COOKIE: Gran used to bash the chickens on the head down Sidcup. We could hit her with a stone.

MAC: Best not do that Cooks.

COOKIE: They don't feel nothing – that's what Gran said.

MAC: Well Gran was a fucking liar Cooks, wasn't she, we both know that. We can't go bashing some woman's head in with a stone.

DECCY: So what we gonna do, leave her, bash her, or take her with us?

RORY: I must have drunk half of that whiskey and I was walking down the ring road singing fucking country music and, you know, I love, really really *love* westerns. American films. Diners. Deserts. And when I wake up I'm in this fucking field, I've got a bleeding lip, eye out to fucking here and my wallet's gone...

COOKIE: It takes two of us to hold onto the pole thing and Mac's got the saw…

DECCY: It aint fucking woodwork man…

MAC: I got to push it aint I?

COOKIE: She doesn't make no noise though I can see her looking at me, just lies there…

MAC: (*Sawing.*) She's still fucking dead man, whatever you say…

DECCY: Fucks sake Mac, watch me fingers…

MAC: Got a chest like a fucking kebab…

COOKIE: Then Deccy says…

DECCY: Ruined her jumper she has……

MAC stops sawing. They look at each other.

MAC: Deccy, get the laptop.

DECCY: Will I get the Play Station?

MAC: Get the fucking lot.

MAC and COOKIE pick up STELLA and put her on the camp bed from the boot of the car with a bit of the pole still sticking out of her. DECCY comes over the hedge laden down with stuff from the car.

COOKIE: She's heavy, aint she?

MAC: Fucks sake Dec, aint you going to help?

DECCY: I got to carry all this.

COOKIE: And it started to rain again.

The boys stand with STELLA on the stretcher between them, looking at the rain.

JEAN: Kick boxing is the best man. Any bloke or girl touches me I'll kick the backside off them.

TERRY: What's that – over there?

JEANIE: My mum broke this bloke's nose once. Electricity man he was. Punched straight in the face. We had a right laugh.

TERRY: Jeans?

JEAN: A girl got to protect herself. I aint never liked girly stuff. Waste of time. You got to have respect. There's this girl, Charnese…down the Bancroft. Six foot tall, backside the size of Tesco's car park, chains hanging off her like a fucking Christmas tree. Her Auntie's got the Nail Studio on the High Street. She's got fucking nails with Gareth on one week and Miss Dynamite the next. Anyway, we're in the sit down chip shop up Lee and this right rough skinhead sees her nails and says 'Miss Dynamite's a fucking slag,' right in Charnese's face like, so she puts her chips down, I aint kidding ya, and kick boxes the skinhead out the door. On his hands and knees he was. Then she comes back, sprinkles her saveloy with vinegar and says 'You all got to learn kickboxing, aint you girls – cause it's kind to your nails.'

TERRY runs his hand over a bush. Looks at it.

TERRY: Shit.

TERRY spreads his fingers out, smells them.

Jeans? Jeanie? It's fucking…white. It's all over everything and it's fucking…white.

MAC, DECCY and COOKIE are walking with the stretcher.

DECCY: You got to stop mate. Can't see where I'm going can I?

MAC: Come on Decs…

DECCY: No I got something…what is this Mac? I got dirt or something in me face.

COOKIE: Looked like a snowman or something he did. We all did. We was all covered in it. Never even saw it coming. Then all of a sudden we was all white. Like ghosts.

TERRY: Fucks sake Jeanie. Fucks sake. It had to fucking happen today.

JEAN: We got to find the car Tes.

TERRY: Don't you get it. We're out here in a field, the war's started and we're contaminated and I've left me fucking gas mask in the fucking fucking car.

JEAN looks at him. Looks around. Looks at her hands. They are white.

Scene Two

COOKIE sits in an old rusty corrugated barn.

The wounded woman is on the floor and MAC is piling up old tables, crates and old barrels.

COOKIE: There was sounds, like thunder, far away. Mac said…

MAC: Could be an earthquake or something…

DECCY: In fucking London?

MAC: Could be.

DECCY: Hey Mac, maybe we're the only ones left alive…

COOKIE: Animals started coming…scared they was, of the water, and the strangeness of everything…chickens, the birds was awake, making noises, and the rats they climbed up onto the shelves to get away from the water…

MAC: Here Dec, give us a hand mate, we got to lift her up, aint we…

MAC and DECCY put STELLA on the next level up.

DECCY: She still aint fucking dead.

They look at her. The rain falls.

MAC: It aint our fault, is it?

DECCY: What aint?

MAC: We was only trying to help her.

DECCY: What you mean?

MAC: I don't want to be mixed up with no dead woman. They'll think we done it.

DECCY: No. We'll find a phone, won't we? Let them know where she is.

MAC: Yeah.

COOKIE: It's dark but we find these lamp things and we look up… Mac, there's this cat, up in the roof, looking down. I see it and it calls to me, glad we're here, cause, I'm not kidding you, we was all dead scared.

RORY: I've lost my watch but it's late… I start walking because I have no idea where the fuck I am and I am up to my ankles in mud, it's like something – biblical – and then I'm in this field, fuck knows where, I can't even see the edges…

TERRY: We got to find shelter aint we? In case they nuke us.

JEAN: And where are we meant to do that? There aint anything here Tes.

TERRY: I aint messing around here Jeans. If we get nuked, and we're like just out in it, we're gonna be fucking lucky if we die. I mean, they could drop fucking anything on us. Fucking botulism.

JEAN: Will you give it a rest Tel.

TERRY: I aint messing about here Jeanie. What you think this is?

JEAN: I dunno do I?

TERRY: Antrax.

JEAN: Fuck off.

TERRY looks at her.

If this was fucking antrax we'd all be dead.

TERRY: Not for three days we wouldn't.

Beat.

JEAN: You are so full of shit.

TERRY: You do what you like, Jeans, alright? Piss off home, go for a fucking country walk, but I'm going to find shelter.

They look at each other.

RORY: This bloke at work today – he has this baby. Always fucking banging on about this baby. How being a father was the best thing in the world, only fucking thing that mattered. Couldn't talk to him about anything but he'd work it round to the baby. See that thing on the telly last night – yeah mate, I was just feeding Jack…seen the football…wanted to but Jack was teething…what do you reckon to Saddam fucking Hussein then– thing is mate, when you're a father, changes your attitude doesn't it? So, two years on the kid gets leukaemia and this bloke, he comes in today -and we're in the middle of a case conference with Sally and he stands there and he says, I killed my kid. Just like that. And after we've all picked ourselves up off the floor Sally's making him tea and Orlando's calling the police and telling them to be sensitive, and I'm looking at him hoping it's true, cause even though I hate the fucking bastard, it takes courage to put someone you love out of their misery, to relieve their suffering and I found myself – respecting him for it. Thinking he was lucky – to have had the chance.

DECCY: You hear something out there?

MAC listens. COOKIE sits with a chicken on his lap.

Sounds like there's someone out there.

They listen.

COOKIE: Mac? Mac?

They listen.

MAC: Who's going be out here at this time of night?

COOKIE: I was thinking, we're like Noah and the ark aint we?

MAC: How d'you mean Cookie?

COOKIE: Sitting here. It's like the flood. Maybe we're the only ones left. You me, Deccy, the wounded lady. We got chickens and a cat, mice. Maybe it'll rain for a long time, and then…when it's over…there'll be just us.

MAC, DECCY, COOKIE, RORY, TERRY and JEAN listen to the rain falling and the distant thunder.

The chickens cluck.

Scene Three

The sound of torrential rain.

RORY arrives, a chicken under his arm.

RORY: About two o'clock in the morning I find this chicken and it starts to follow me. I tell it to get lost but ten minutes later I turn around and there it is, still right behind me. Clucking. We get to this really flooded part, I'm wading through, and the chicken – flaps over, can't quite make it, skims the surface of the muddy water – looks at me. So, I pick it up. It's warm. I put my coat around it, shield it. I can feel its heart beating. Then for a minute, the clouds clear, blown off by the wind, and there's this moment of light.

COOKIE: Mac's standing there, rubbing his arms, trying to get warm, when this light comes in through all the cracks in the barn – cracked up and broken boards everywhere there was, and Deccy looks up…

DECCY: Who's turned the fucking overheads on?

MAC: You knobhead you. That's moonlight, aint it.

DECCY: Fuck off.

MAC: You aint never seen moonlight? You wanker.

COOKIE: And Dec's just looking – up – he says he aint never noticed it before – not down the Laurels anyhow.

MAC (*Looking at the wounded woman.*) We should of left her there.

DECCY breaks away and picks up the laptop.

DECCY: (*Opening the laptop.*) What you reckon this is worth Mac?

MAC: (*Still looking.*) Taken the stuff and fucking legged it.

DECCY: Three hundred – maybe more.

COOKIE: She's got this medal on.

MAC and DECCY come over to look. COOKIE shows them the medal.

DECCY: Silver is it?

MAC: St Christopher.

DECCY: You what?

MAC: Nan had one. St Christopher. Looks after you like. For travellers.

DECCY: He's done a fucking crap job tonight then, aint he?

They can't help laughing.

What's that then?

DECCY goes over to a box in the barn. Has a look inside.

Fucks sake – it's only fucking rum – bottles of it.

MAC and COOKIE go over. DECCY opens a bottle. Takes a drink.

Fucking brilliant this is.

He offers the others a drink. MAC takes a deep swig.

MAC: (*Appreciating it.*) Shit. Fucking hell.

COOKIE drinks.

COOKIE: It's dead nice. Warm. Makes you feel better right away. I give the lady some. She drinks it.

MAC: What you doing you knobhead?

COOKIE: That's what you got to do. I seen it on the telly.

DECCY: This on *National Rescue* was it?

COOKIE: She's breathing.

MAC: Fucks sake. What did I tell you? We should of left her.

RORY is walking with the chicken.

RORY: So I start telling this chicken…how things are. How I'm leaving home when I get mugged, and how I'm lost and that chicken's just snuggled up inside my coat and I'm thinking, this is nice. Nicer than anything I ever had with Rachel, and then it hits me, that I am happier with this chicken, a strange chicken, than I have ever been in my relationship. I look into her black eyes, and I see something there. Honest to God, I see something there I've not seen since Margate, 1975 – I see something… looking back at me. Not just that it's alive – something that is…really…conscious. Looking back at me. Fragile. And I think of my dad, talking about – how we should be, giving one of his up-your-ass speeches…going on about…stewardship…stewardship. And I'm holding this chicken under my coat and thinking about my dad, standing there in the Battersea Rise Social Club, his yellow fingers wrapped round an oily pint and talking at me through the thick air, about…fucking…stewardship.

TERRY: We're going North, right?

JEAN: No we aint.

TERRY: Is this a fucking compass I'm holding or what?

JEAN: You wearing your NYPD Police badge are you?

TERRY: What's that got to do with anything?

JEAN: Give us the torch.

TERRY: It was my idea to bring the torch.

JEAN: That mean you got to fucking wave it about all night does it?

JEAN takes the torch.

Give us the compass.

She takes it off him.

North – over there.

TERRY: It aint.

JEAN: You put a compass up to your chest and you're wearing metal it attracts don't it? Far as this compass is concerned North's anywhere your fucking chest is.

TERRY looks at the compass, looks at his police badge under his shirt.

You hear that?

TERRY: Fucks sake.

They listen.

JEAN: Baby crying.

They listen.

TERRY: Where you going…

JEAN: Following the sound aint I?

The baby cries.

TERRY: Fucking baby, lying in this ditch.

Back at the barn. MAC and DECCY are swigging the rum.

DECCY: See the way that big bloke looked at you, fucking ace man.

MAC: 'We heard as how you was dealing down the Laurels…'

DECCY: (*As MAC.*) 'That right mate – want something do you?' Fucking brilliant.

MAC: Wanker.

DECCY: You serious – Mac – about not going back?

MAC drinks.

COOKIE: Mac?

DECCY: Cause – if you wasn't going back – then – I dunno – maybe – I dunno – I think I'd go with you man. Yeah, I think I would.

COOKIE: Mac? What's he on about?

MAC: Nothing. Forget it Cooks.

DECCY: Fucking shit hole. If I never saw the Laurels one more time I wouldn't give a toss.

COOKIE: You going away?

DECCY: Take Cooks with us. See Cookie – (*He drinks.*) I'm going to be this Eddie Micheals, and Mac here's…what is it – Dimetreo – fucking…something Greek.

COOKIE: You going Mac?

MAC: I aint going nowhere without you Cooks. (*To DECCY.*) Why don't you just shut up?

COOKIE: I thought you was going somewhere Mac.

MAC: Not without you Cookie. What you take me for?

COOKIE: Mac was there when I was born Deccy. Did I tell you that?

DECCY: Yeah Cookie, you told me.

COOKIE: Saw me come out.

MAC: Right ugly bastard.

COOKIE: Mac's sitting now, drinking that rum, he's got blood on his chin, and the cat moves down, right down it comes, from up the top and sits on his lap. Tell the story Mac.

MAC: Not now Cooks.

COOKIE: Our mum was working, wasn't she Mac – down Iceland – and she's got these…pains to say I'm coming but she says babies take their time, and she aint hardly home from Iceland like when…

MAC: She's sitting down on the fucking carpet man…

COOKIE: Mac was five, wasn't you Mac…

MAC: And she's – like –

DECCY: What man?

MAC: Me mum – she's like – having him, knobhead over there…

DECCY: In front of you?

MAC: Yeah.

DECCY: You seen him come out?

MAC: Yeah.

DECCY: That's gross man.

COOKIE: I come out me foot first…

MAC: Thought he was a fucking footballer didn't we…

COOKIE: That's what my mum says, cause of me coming out foot first…

DECCY: Didn't you call no doctor?

MAC: Wasn't time was there? Then, after a bit…

COOKIE: Me bottom come out…

DECCY: Don't tell me no more Cooks, alright… (*He drinks.*)

COOKIE: Mac held mum's hand, didn't you Mac…

MAC: We lived down Peters Street then, and this bloke, next door, he was always hitting on the wall with this sledgehammer – anything got up his nose he'd hit the wall with this fucking…big…sledgehammer, so he's giving it fuck knows what, hitting on the wall, and Mum says…

COOKIE: Go next door and tell Mr Sweeny your brother's having a fit.

DECCY: Fucks sake, why'd she want you to do that?

COOKIE: She was that clever mum, wasn't she Mac?

MAC: Didn't want him to know she was having a baby, did she?

DECCY: Why not?

COOKIE: Case he killed me. Cause he killed this boy in these flats in Sheffield didn't he Mac, cause he used to play his guitar.

MAC: Couldn't stand babies, could he, Mr Sweeny.

DECCY: You go tell him then?

MAC: Yeah. 'Having a fit? I'll give him a fucking fit,' he says, 'if he don't shut the fuck up.'

COOKIE: But it didn't matter, did it Mac, cause I was out by then.

MAC: Yeah. That's right. You was out.

JEAN approaches a bush.

JEAN: It is a baby.

TERRY: Come on Jeans.

JEANIE: I aint kidding you. There's a baby down there.

TERRY: 'Bout three months old it was. Dead wet from the rain.

JEAN: How'd it get here?

TERRY: Fucks sake, I don't know.

JEAN: Maybe someone's dumped it.

She stares at it.

Must be. Someone's come out here and left it, aint they.

TERRY: Yeah.

JEAN: Best take it with us.

TERRY: Yeah.

JEAN goes to pick it up.

Only Jeanie – thing is…

JEAN: What?

TERRY: I dunno. If someone left it, they don't want it – do they?

JEAN: Maybe they don't want it…

TERRY: We take it, shows we been out here.

JEAN: Yeah? And?

TERRY: We got the Social after us – the police – we bring back a baby, there's gonna be questions aint there?

JEAN: We can't leave it here – can we?

TERRY: I'm just saying – we got to think.

Jeanie looks.

44

JEAN: They're going to put it in Care aint they?

TERRY: Maybe someone – loves it.

JEAN: Can't be. Don't stand to reason do it? If someone loved it, wouldn't have been dumped, would it?

TERRY: Maybe the mum's…I dunno – just lost it or something. I aint saying nothing – just that we got to think. I nicked that car – didn't I?

JEAN: So?

TERRY: What else you gonna take tonight – eh? What if we find a horse or something – we got to take that home too?

JEAN: This aint a horse – it's a baby.

Beat.

It aint right – just to leave it.

TERRY: They'll want to know – how we got it.

JEAN: I'm taking it. Alright? Alright.

JEAN picks up the baby. TERRY looks at her.

COOKIE: It's nearly two in the morning. We was that tired, but it was cold like. We couldn't sleep. Mac looked out the door.

MAC looks out across the land.

DECCY: You think they're still out there Mac?

MAC: Maybe I should go, see if I can find the road.

COOKIE: But we say no. Let's stay together. Deccy passes Mac the rum. Just about then, we notice these sacks.

DECCY: Fucks sake.

DECCY pulls out a piece of gnarled meat.

What you think this is then?

MAC: Chicken is it? Smoked or something.

DECCY: It aint chicken.

COOKIE: We was dead hungry.

DECCY: (*Sniffing it.*) Smells – alright.

MAC: Looks old Dec.

DECCY: FUCK – it's got the – fucking hell – the heads on.

COOKIE : Had this little shrunken head – little teeth.

DECCY: Fucks sake – what *is* that!

MAC: It's…it's …fucking hell man it's a…monkey.

DECCY: Get it away from me man!

MAC: You've been sniffing a fucking monkey man.

MAC looks inside the rest of the sacks.

Look Deccy – there's a whole fucking bag of them.

DECCY: Who eats monkeys?

COOKIE: I seen it on the telly. Bushmeat. It's from Africa or someplace. They catch it in the jungle.

DECCY: Get rid of it man. I don't want it near me.

MAC shows the others a hunk of meat.

MAC: You know what this is?

DECCY: Take us to end up with a load of dead fucking monkeys.

MAC: It's stuff what someone's stashed. It's knock off, aint it?

DECCY: Knock off monkeys? That's gross man. I'm telling you Mac I'm gonna chuck up, I know I am.

MAC: We could sell this.

DECCY: You are kidding me? Where we gonna sell that, down Tescos – excuse me mister, you want to buy a bag full of knock off monkeys? Do us a favour.

MAC: You got to sell it down markets. Down Brixton. That's where you sell it.

COOKIE: I seen it on the telly. You can get gazelles and all sorts.

DECCY: Fucking gazelles? Oh yeah, I forgot, that's me sister's favourite…gazelle and chips.

MAC: Don't know a good deal when you see it.

COOKIE picks up the monkey carcass.

COOKIE: Poor monkey. Poor boy.

MAC: Don't fancy eating it then Cooks? I'm fucking starving.

COOKIE wraps up the monkey carcass in his scarf.

COOKIE: They kiss they do, monkeys.

DECCY: This one don't.

COOKIE: (*Stroking the dead monkey.*) They aint that different from us, are they?

DECCY: Not from you anyhows.

MAC: (*Grabbing DECCY.*) What the fuck's that meant to mean?

DECCY: It was only a joke Mac.

MAC: It aint funny.

DECCY: Sorry Mac – alright?

MAC stares at DECCY, holding him by the neck of his sweatshirt. MAC lets go.

JEAN: We could keep it.

TERRY: You what?

JEAN: Say it was ours.

TERRY: You lost it or what?

JEAN: How could they tell it aint our baby?

TERRY: I don't know Jeans – DNA – birth certificate, your mum happening to say you aint never been pregnant.

JEAN: No one wants it. Why shouldn't we have it? Look after it. I could really love it.

TERRY: You're fifteen Jeanie. You been in eight foster homes and two residential centres and you aint got no training in nothing.

JEAN: Don't need no training to work in Tescos.

TERRY: I don't believe I'm hearing this. That baby's got to belong to someone.

JEAN: They aint got a right to it though – have they? Not after this. The way I see it is, we saved it – didn't we Tes?

TERRY: You got to put it back now Jeans and we got to go home.

JEAN: Thing is , we don't know how to get home no more. You know what I think? I think this is like the one chance you get. You get like one chance in your life to do something. This night is our chance. We don't go back do we? We just keep on walking away. Away from Peters Street, away from London, keep going till we get to a place where no one aint never seen us before. Then, when we get there, we start again. Just you me, and this baby. We just got to start walking, and not stop till we're there.

RORY arrives at the wreck of the car.

RORY: Half an hour later and I'm walking – wishing that this bird could tell me – explain to me – its feelings. I know that it's got something to say. I'm ready to hear it. And I think of that man down Margate with the monkey in the little red jumper. He'd put it on your shoulder for fifty pence. Its tiny feet, its tiny brown toes curling around your jacket to steady itself and my dad always made us – wouldn't take no for an answer – come on – you got to have your picture taken with the monkey – and Mum – looking the other way – looking out to sea – and the smell of the chip vinegar burning the back of your throat – come on Rory – look – here's the monkey – and talking to that monkey in my head – saying over and over – in my head – I'm sorry – I'm sorry – I'm sorry. The rain's coming in thin sheets now. Me and the chicken we climb up over this kissing gate – it's a nice idea – a kissing gate – it's like climbing up into a time tunnel – one foot up and I'm thinking kissing – other foot up and I'm seeing Susan Halliday – one foot down and I've got the suede of her cowboy jacket under the palm of my right hand, other foot down – I'm back, I'm here, I'm grown up – and she's gone. The chicken buries its head in my armpit – and I see the car for the first time, rolled over, windscreen shattered, end up in a ditch.

RORY approaches the car.

JEAN wraps the baby up. TERRY looks at the horizon.

TERRY: We still got to get out of here.

JEAN: If you don't want to go with me, that's alright.

TERRY looks at her.

TERRY: Come on. We got to find the road.

MAC: (*Looking at STELLA.*) You think there's something we should do?

DECCY: What d'you mean?

MAC: Don't seem right, just leaving her there.

MAC kneels down beside STELLA.

You gone through her pockets?

DECCY: I got the purse.

MAC searches through STELLA's pockets. He takes out a dummy.

What you found?

COOKIE looks.

MAC: Fucks sake.

DECCY: What is it Mac? What you got?

MAC: You know what this means – don't you?

DECCY and COOKIE stare.

There's a baby out there.

DECCY: Didn't hear no baby crying.

COOKIE: A baby?

DECCY: It's pissing down with rain Mac. If there is a baby – it's been out there – hours.

MAC: Don't matter. Could still be alive.

DECCY: What you on about now?

MAC: We got to get it, don't we?

DECCY: Do we?

MAC: We got to look.

DECCY: We don't have to do nothing. One wet night in the middle of fuck knows where, some woman we aint never seen before and her kid get killed on the road. What's that got to do with us Mac? If we'd walked the other way we wouldn't have seen nothing. Kids die every day up the Laurels, we don't go looking for them. You tell him Cookie, would you?

COOKIE: Mac takes the St Christopher off the lady. He puts it round his neck.

RORY: And I'm actually thinking – if I could get this car started – I'd just fucking drive…

COOKIE: And he looks at me, and for a minute, he don't look like Mac, looks like Mum…

RORY: I'm tired, and it's warm out of the wind, so I put the chicken on the passenger seat, on top of the roadmap…slide down a ways…close my eyes…

MAC: I'll be back.

COOKIE: And next thing, there's just me, and Deccy, and the dead monkeys, and the sound of the wind, and the rain.

Scene Four

RORY: So I'm having this dream – it's raining – and in the dream I'm a kid again, and I'm under this candlewick bedspread that I used to pull the tufty bits out of and I always thought one day it would go totally bald, but Tom would say that my candlewick bedspread was the only one in Walthamstow that grew new hair at night and that's why no matter how much stuff I pulled out it would never go bald, and he's sitting there, on the bed, in his football boots and the rain's coming down and I'm thinking, it's so good to see you mate, Tom, my brother, it's so good to see you, and he's looking at me and grinning and then I think, but you're dead. Aren't you dead? And I say to him, how'd you get here Tom, you're dead, and he says, I came back to you inside your fire truck, and I'm thinking, that fire truck – cause I had this fire truck with a flashing light and he used to push it round the kitchen floor doing the voices for the two plastic firemen inside – Saying – watch out Dave you'll never take that corner, and put your foot down Geoff, it's a big buggering fire, and they were called Dave and Geoff those little men and whenever he said buggering fire it made me wet my pants laughing which is why he said it, and I was thinking, how did you get inside that fire truck Tom because you're too big, aren't you, you're too big and he said when you're dead you can fit into anywhere.

MAC is standing beside the car. Suddenly RORY opens his eyes – sees MAC. They stare at each other.

MAC: Fucks sake.

COOKIE: It's only his fucking Social worker.

RORY: Alan MacKenna.

MAC: What you doing here Mr Wilson?

They look at each other.

RORY: I was lost. Got mugged…no, let's get this right, got pissed, *then* I got mugged, and next thing I know I'm out here, not here exactly, somewhere, and, I start walking and then I see this car and…I got inside.

MAC: You got a mobile?

RORY: They took it.

MAC: You heard anything?

RORY: What kind of thing?

MAC: There's a baby out here somewhere and we got to find it.

COOKIE: When the tree come down it made a right noise. Shook everything. We didn't never see it till the morning so we didn't know what is was just then. Deccy stood right up, listening. Waiting for it to come again, but we didn't hear nothing after that. Not for a time anyhows.

RORY: You brought a baby out here?

MAC: There was this woman, in the car.

RORY: In this car?

MAC: Ended up in the hedge over there, had to cut her out of it, then we see she's got one of them dummy things what kids suck on, so it stands to reason, don't it? Must have been a baby.

RORY: Where is she – the woman?

MAC: Back at the barn. She aint gonna last long but we aint got no mobiles have we, so we can't do nothing.

RORY: Christ.

MAC: You look that side, I'll look in the ditch.

COOKIE: 'Bout twenty minutes after the tree falls there's this noise outside.

DECCY: What the fuck's that?

COOKIE: Could be a wild animal Dec. Dec, I'm scared – don't look.

DECCY picks up a stout stick.

DECCY: You hide over there Cooks – might be someone that aint so friendly.

DECCY and COOKIE take cover. TERRY and JEAN come into the barn with the baby.

JEAN: Aint too bad. It aint Tes. We can dry off here, wait til morning.

DECCY comes out of the shadows with his stick. He blinds TERRY and JEAN with the beam from his torch.

DECCY: Where the fuck do you think you're going?

TERRY: Alright mate – alright.

DECCY: I said, this is our place, alright?

TERRY: Looks pretty big to me.

JEAN: We just come in out of the rain. Great tree nearly fell over and killed us right outside.

DECCY: Fuck me. Jeanie Roach. I thought you was banged up in Care.

TERRY: Declan Walsh?

DECCY: You fucking bastard Terry. Your brother just drove us out here and kicked the shit out of us.

COOKIE steps forward into the light. DECCY and COOKIE look at TERRY and JEAN.

TERRY: That's my brother mate. It aint nothing to do with me.

DECCY: Aint it?

COOKIE: Mac's coming back soon.

TERRY: Is he?

COOKIE: You've got a nice baby.

JEAN: She's cold.

COOKIE: Poor baby. Poor girl.

TERRY: Thought maybe we could, dry out a bit.

DECCY: Oh yeah? That's nice.

TERRY: Won't be long, will we Jeans?

JEAN: Aint good for a baby, being out in the cold.

COOKIE: Are you the mummy?

JEAN looks at TERRY.

JEAN: Yeah. I am.

TERRY: Have a heart mate. We're all in the same boat, aint we?

DECCY: How do you make that out then?

TERRY: You're contaminated…like us.

DECCY: You what?

TERRY: That stuff on your face. We're under attack, aint we? Osama. That's chemical warfare that is, eating away at you. That's why we got to stay inside, take shelter.

COOKS: Mac's outside.

DECCY: You are fucking full of shit, you know that.

COOKIE: Mac's looking for a baby.

DECCY: You think I'm a fucking knobhead or what?

TERRY: I don't think nothing Deccy. All I'm saying is, we got to stick together, and we got to stay inside.

JEAN: Tes, there's someone over here.

TERRY goes over and looks.

TERRY: Fucks sake. What the fuck happened to her?

DECCY: Found her.

TERRY and JEAN look at each other.

She still breathing?

TERRY kneels down.

TERRY: Just about.

DECCY: Aint you got a mobile?

TERRY: Must have fell out of me pocket. Had to climb over the wall up the Claydon.

DECCY: You broke into the Claydon?

TERRY: Know it do you?

DECCY: Put me cousin in there – used to lock him in his room at night.

JEAN: They still do that.

DECCY: Knelt on his chest so hard they busted his ribs.

TERRY: Alright now is he?

DECCY: Put him in a bedsit when he was sixteen.

TERRY: Lucky bugger.

DECCY: He's mental now.

Beat.

JEAN: We're going away, aint we Tes?

TERRY: Gonna try.

COOKIE: I want to go home. I want to go home Dec.

DECCY: We got to wait for Mac, aint we Cooks? (*To TERRY.*) You got any money then?

TERRY: What's that got to do with anything?

DECCY: We aint a charity are we? You want to stay, you got to pay rent.

TERRY: Do me a favour?

DECCY: You don't pay, you got to clear off.

COOKIE: (*Looking at the baby.*) What's her name?

JEAN looks at TERRY.

JEAN: Alexandra. Alex. We call her Al.

COOKIE: I was born on the floor at my house. My mum had Mac put the radio on and I come out on the floor. I come out foot first. Thought I was a footballer.

TERRY: Play football do you?

DECCY: Forget about the fucking football, you gonna pay up or what?

TERRY: Listen mate, all we want to do is stay a couple of hours, til the rain stops. We aint got much money and what we got, we need, alright?

COOKIE: It's like Joseph and Mary aint it Dec? Coming to the Inn in Bethlehem.

TERRY: (*Looking at the injured woman.*) She aint looking so good now.

COOKIE: Then we noticed, the lady from the car, she was breathing so quiet, you couldn't hardly hear it no more.

JEAN: You think we should say a prayer or something?

TERRY: Don't know no prayers.

DECCY: She don't even know what's happening to her.

COOKIE: We could say Nan's prayer.

DECCY: I thought I asked you if you was paying?

TERRY rummages in his pocket. Gives DECCY a five pound note.

Five quid, what's this meant to be…a joke?

TERRY advances on DECCY.

TERRY: You aint getting no more. I got to keep what I got. We got things we got to pay for, aint we?

COOKIE: The Lord is my shepherd, I shall not want, he maketh me to lie down in green pastures, he leadeth me beside the still waters – he restoreth my soul.

TERRY: He does what?

COOKIE: He restoreth my soul.

TERRY: What the fuck does that mean?

COOKIE: Dunno.

DECCY: It's restores – innit? Restores – like…a car.

TERRY: (*Looking at DECCY.*) Yeah. Right.

With RORY and MAC.

MAC: Them ditches are full up with water now.

RORY: Must have got worse while I was asleep. Took a look over there, the water's deep.

MAC: I got to get back to Cookie.

They look at each other.

You gonna be alright then?

RORY: Course.

MAC goes to leave. He stops, turns.

MAC: What you standing there for?

RORY looks at him.

Aint you going home?

RORY: Yeah. Course I am.

RORY reaches into the car and collects the chicken. MAC looks at him.

MAC: You know which way to go?

They look at each other.

You better come with me then.

JEAN: The thing about babies is you got to keep them clean, fed and love them. And not shout.

DECCY: I'll fucking shout if it starts crying.

JEAN: Down our flats we got a woman screamed that much at her kid me mum went down the social and said she'd only gone and got an asthma attack cause the screaming was that bad, her nerves was in a right state, and it weren't only in the day, it was all night too. My bedroom's beside that little boy's room, so where I am I can hear everything, so night time I'm lying in bed, pillow over me head, cause of the noise, and this little boy he's like, crying his heart out and the mum she must be, I don't know, smashing stuff all over the bedroom calling him names and saying like she's going to smash his head in if he don't shut the fuck up, and his screaming, it starts to go like, really REALLY high, and you can tell when that happens that she must have got hold of him, and, the only thing it's like, you know what it's like, it's like when them Pinder boys killed that cat, it made a noise like that, really, really…high it was. Later on, I'd lie in bed and whisper, let's pray to God eh? Let's pray to God. After about three hours of screaming, the baby screaming and the mum screaming and swearing, it'd go dead quiet. I reckon she went out then, left him in

59

there alone. She'd go out when that bloke come over. That fat bloke. Leave the baby alone. Bet that baby was dead glad. When she went out. I was six then.

RORY: What're you doing out here Mac?

MAC: Got beat up, didn't we?

RORY: Who did that to you?

MAC: It aint none of your business, is it?

MAC stops abruptly.

It's still out there. The fucking baby.

RORY: We looked.

MAC: Got to get back to Cookie.

MAC turns on RORY.

I don't want no trouble when we get there, alright? No questions or nothing? And it aint none of your business what's in that place.

RORY: Listen – mate – I couldn't give a toss what's there as long as it's dry.

MAC: There's fucking dead monkeys. Fucking sacks of them.

RORY: You sure you didn't get a knock on the head Mac?

MAC: Cookie's there – he's scared aint he?

RORY: Right.

TERRY: After an hour – maybe a bit longer – Dec says…

DECCY: She's dead.

TERRY: We all just looked. No one said nothing. You don't have to see no one dead before to know what it looks like. Dec, he hadn't seen no one dead, but Cookie had.

COOKIE: Saw my Nan dead I did.

TERRY: And I seen police photos – on the internet – so – I knew what it looked like. They were fucking brilliant photos…all gangland murders and rapes and stuff – didn't have to pay or nothing.

COOKIE: Mum said I could touch her, so I did – she was right cold. I got into her bed.

DECCY: With your dead Nan? Gross.

JEAN: No it aint.

TERRY: Horrible that is.

JEAN: No it aint.

COOKIE: Got into bed with her and put me head on her shoulder like I did when she read to me, only she didn't move no more.

DECCY: She was fucking dead Cooks.

COOKIE: She had a thing in her stomach killed her.

DECCY: Like alien, was it?

COOKIE: She had nice hair. Used to have clips. Give em me sometimes, for me train.

DECCY: We got me dad in a cardboard box in the airing cupboard. Give us his ashes at the crematorium. Had on his football shirt in the coffin. Knocked off his bike he was. Two weeks later mum pours petrol on his bike on the balcony and only fucking sets it on fire. Nearly burns the whole fucking flats down. I wanted that bike. Didn't speak to her for a week. It was me dad's bike. She had no right to fucking burn it up.

JEAN, DECCY, COOKIE and TERRY stare at the body.

TERRY: Looks alright now, don't she?

DECCY: We done our best, didn't we?

TERRY: Course you did.

DECCY: Wasn't like we even knew her or nothing.

TERRY: She have any stuff on her?

DECCY and COOKIE look at each other.

DECCY: What kind of stuff?

TERRY: I don't know. Radio…cash.

COOKIE looks at DECCY.

Oh I get it. Right. You've already cleaned her out.

COOKIE: Mac's coming back soon.

TERRY: We could go halves, eh?

DECCY: Get lost.

TERRY: What you want me to do, tell the Old Bill you only went and cleaned out a dead woman – might not even buy it that you didn't have a hand in knocking her about a bit.

DECCY: What the fuck do you mean by that?

MAC appears in the doorway.

MAC: Yeah – what do you mean by that?

TERRY: Mac, mate. Didn't mean nothing.

RORY comes in holding his chicken.

COOKIE: Then this bloke comes in, with a chicken. Turns out he's Mac's social worker. He's got a chicken and all, so I says to him, what's the name of your chicken? And he says…

RORY: She hasn't got a name.

COOKIE: Then Mac sees the lady from the car.

MAC: She dead then?

DECCY: Yeah.

COOKIE: We said a prayer.

MAC: Good.

COOKIE: There was this big noise then, it was like…

DECCY: Like a great wall falling down someplace far away…

TERRY: Like a bomb going off…

JEAN: Like a great weight falling…

COOKIE: And Mac said…

MAC: The water's coming.

Scene Five

RORY, JEAN and COOKIE sit on the roof of the barn.

RORY makes a roll up. Hands it to JEAN. Starts making one for himself.

RORY: How come you got stuck out here?

JEAN: What's it to you?

JEAN lights the roll up and rocks the baby.

COOKIE: You've got a chicken.

RORY: Yes…

COOKIE: What's its name?

RORY: It doesn't have a name.

COOKIE takes a closer look at RORY's chicken.

COOKIE: It's got nice eyes.

RORY: Yeah. It has.

JEAN: Water must be six foot deep. Saw a dead sheep go by a while back.

COOKIE: Poor sheep. Poor boy.

RORY: Soon it'll stop.

JEAN: What if it don't?

They all look out across the water.

RORY: They must know there's people stranded out here.

DECCY climbs up through a hole in the roof.

DECCY: Aint no good Cooks…we couldn't get that woman up the ladder, could we?

MAC climbs up after him.

MAC: It's fucking cold in that water.

MAC slings the last of the stolen valuables onto the roof.

JEAN: Where's Terry?

DECCY: Went after some sacking…up the other end.

JEAN: And you didn't go with him?

DECCY: He didn't want no one to go with him.

JEAN: You should of helped him.

DECCY: He's the fucking army cadet.

RORY: You got the lamp then?

DECCY: Now we got a fucking social worker and all.

MAC: That water's gone deep. It's half way up the door.

They all look.

JEAN: You got to go down there and look for him.

DECCY: You go.

JEAN: I got the baby.

RORY: I'll go.

DECCY: Take your time.

RORY climbs down the ladder.

COOKIE: I seen her jumper first…cause it was white like.

DECCY: A fucking social worker…what's he going to say about us when he gets back?

COOKIE: Her eyes was open, looking at the moon…

MAC: He won't say nothing, cause if he does I'll tell them he buys shit off me down the Laurels…

COOKIE: Floating out across the black water, round and away, round and away…

MAC: They find out he's been buying shit off me, he's dead, aint he?

COOKIE: That lady's gone.

They all stand on the roof to get a better look. They look down into the water for a long time.

JEAN: (*Rocking the baby to herself.*) Water must have lifted her up.

They all watch the body being swept away on the current. TERRY climbs up through the roof.

TERRY: There's all sorts up the back there. Loads of boxes…radios, fucking DVDs…

JEAN: You serious?

TERRY: Put em up the top where the water won't get em.

DECCY: That's our stuff you're messing with.

TERRY: No it aint. Don't give me that crap.

TERRY gives JEAN some sacking...they wrap it round themselves.

COOKIE: You think we're gonna drown Mac?

Everyone looks out across the water. RORY climbs up.

RORY: (*To TERRY.*) I was looking for you.

TERRY: I was here mate.

RORY: We thought something must have happened to you.

DECCY: Pity it didn't.

TERRY opens a bottle of rum. Drinks from it. Passes it to JEAN. She drinks.

What you think you're doing?

TERRY: Get stuffed will you?

TERRY drinks again. The others look at him. He passes the bottle to RORY who drinks, RORY passes it to DECCY and MAC.

There's this place, round the back of the betting shop on the High Street, full of fucking shit, dog shit, piss, needles, my dad goes down the betting shop, Saturday morning, slips inside, into the smoke, like a fucking hero going down the tunnel at Millwall, slips inside from the High Street...fag ends, betting slips, telly blaring...

JEAN: (*To the baby.*) Need a park babies do, one of them parks with baby swings.

TERRY: Alright Barry mate, alright you wanker you, fancy a pint, fucking hell – five race accumulator...fucking lucky bastard...come here...pencil on thin paper, here's a betting slip son, draw a picture eh?... Strike a match...

sulphur burning at the back of your throat…and they're off, thud thud thud thud thud…and they're off…

JEAN: Push to the sky, down we go, push to the sky and down we go…look at the squirrel, isn't he nice, he's looking at you, want to feed him, give him a nut, back on the swings, and push to the sky…

COOKIE: Squirrels save their food till winter…bury it.

JEAN: Push to the sky –

COOKIE: Colin Pinder shot a squirrel down the Laurels with an air gun…

JEAN: Push to the sky…

COOKIE: Bit of his head went on the wall…

JEAN: Push to the sky…

COOKIE: Chucked him in the bin outside Tescos…

TERRY: Alright Barry mate, this your boy…

COOKIE: Picked it out I did, went back and got that little tiny bit of its head…

TERRY: So I'm round the back of that betting shop…

COOKIE: In a bit of tinfoil I did…

TERRY: Quiet it was, all overgrown…

COOKIE: Wrapped him up in Nan's old tea towel…

TERRY: Traffic over the wall…and the race on the telly spilling out the back door…

COOKIE: Can't dig no holes in the park, not allowed…

TERRY: There's that much shit…

COOKIE: So I go down the back of the betting shop with Nan's big spoon…

TERRY: Puss eyed dog, staring at me, shitting…

COOKIE: It's nice there. Quiet. Sound of the telly spilling out the back door…

TERRY: Give it a bit of chocolate, licks my hand…

COOKIE: Dig a hole right by the wall

(*Sings.*) The day thou gavest Lord has ended
The darkness falls at thy behest…

TERRY: Dad comes out… What happened to fucking luck eh? When God was handing out the good fucking luck son I must have been behind the shed, you know what I mean?

COOKIE: Buried it in the long green grass. Made a cross. Poor boy. Poor squirrel.

JEAN: They don't need much…babies…the way I see it. You just got to love them and keep them clean.

COOKIE: Nan singing on a Saturday night on the balcony…

JEAN: That's all they need the way I see it.

COOKIE: (*Sings.*) To thee our morning hymns ascended… Thy praise shall sanctify our rest.

Beat.

RORY: (*Calling.*) Can anyone hear us?

DECCY: You want someone to come do you?

RORY: Don't you?

DECCY: Not his fucking brother I don't. Want to go home…to your nice flat?

RORY: I'm not going home.

DECCY: Where you going then?

RORY: I don't know. I'm just not...going back.

DECCY: You're so full of shit.

DECCY looks at RORY.

You've got a job aint you?

RORY: I hate my fucking job.

DECCY: How you going to live?

RORY: Don't know.

DECCY: You hear this Mac? Your case worker, he's only having a fucking nervous breakdown. You've only gone and give him a fucking nervous breakdown.

MAC looks at RORY. They start to laugh.

You got money though aint you?

RORY: I owe money. Credit cards, bank loan, everyone. I'm crap with money. Spend it.

DECCY: Yeah?

RORY: (*Drinking the rum.*) Fucking drink it if I can.

DECCY drinks.

DECCY: You ever meet my cousin Si down the Claydon?

MAC looks at RORY – their eyes meet.

JEAN: What's he look like?

DECCY: Right ugly bugger. Six foot two and eight stone nothing. Has a number one hair cut and he looks like a fucking bog brush.

The others drink and snigger.

Put him into care cause he used to cut himself all over. Liked it. His mum used to slap him on the head – 'Don't you fucking cut yourself Simon or I'll put you into care.'

JEAN: Everyone cuts themselves down the Claydon.

DECCY: Had to hide all the knives, scissors, everything.

JEAN: Girl in my room cut herself with a bolt she got off the bookshelves in the library, just…gouged herself.

DECCY: Anyway, he has to talk to this social worker and she says…in their kitchen this is…why do you want to hurt yourself Simon'…and he says (*DECCY is cracking up.*) 'Cause I can't fucking stand meself.' And we're all in the kitchen pissing ourselves, and she says, 'But Simon, you have such a lot to offer' and he's looking at her, waiting for her to tell him *what*…what he's got to offer… and she's digging herself a real hole now, and she says… 'I can see you're a very sensitive boy'…and he says… 'But I aint got any mates. They all just think I'm an ugly bastard.'

DECCY's in fits.

RORY: (*Feeling MAC still watching.*) What did she say?

DECCY laughs and laughs until he pulls himself together.

DECCY: (*Choking, coughing.*) Nothing. Filled in her form and got in her car and drove home to fucking Bromley.

JEAN: I don't think I ever saw him.

DECCY: Ended up in this bedsit. Put him on these drugs to stop him talking to himself.

RORY: I talk to myself.

DECCY: You need drugs mate.

RORY: I wouldn't mind.

DECCY: Tell you what, you can see that lady from Bromley…she'll fix you up.

MAC looks at JEAN.

MAC: Where'd you get that baby?

JEAN glances at TERRY.

How come it's so wet?

JEAN: It *is* fucking raining, or hadn't you noticed?

MAC: That aint your baby, is it?

JEAN: You what?

MAC: They let you keep a baby up the Claydon?

JEAN: Course they do. And it aint none of your business.

TERRY: Yeah. Why don't you shut up Mac?

RORY: How old are you Jeanie?

JEAN: You know something, I think you got to be *perverted* to do what you do? Sticking your nose into people's lives, fucking ABUSING them.

RORY: I thought they only let girls your age keep a baby in a special unit?

JEAN: You saying I stole this baby?

Beat. Everyone looks.

MAC: That's the baby from the car, aint it?

JEAN: Course it aint.

MAC: How come you aint got no baby stuff?

JEAN: I just been broke out of the Claydon, it aint like I had loads of time to pack.

MAC: You can't just take a baby.

JEAN: Just suppose this weren't my baby…which it is…but just suppose this was some dead woman's baby what I found in a ditch. I hadn't seen it, picked it up…it'd be dead right now, from the cold and the rain and all. And don't you go telling me that you can't just take no baby, cause just supposing this was some lost baby…which it aint… I can't see no difference between me picking it up and caring for it and the Social going down me sister Rita's and taking her baby off her cause they say she aint fit, and then putting it in some home where the attendant only goes and fucking touches her up. People take fucking babies all the time, so don't go telling me that people don't take no fucking babies…cause they do.

COOKIE: When the water come up over the door Dec said…

DECCY: You think when we get back home…they'll have…bombed it or something?

COOKIE: Terry went and took something out of his pocket, started chewing on it –

DECCY: Fucking Osama… What've we ever done to him…bastard.

TERRY: Lives in a cave, don't he?

COOKIE: Jesus lived in a cave.

DECCY: Just, all me CDs are back home.

RORY: Thought you weren't going home?

COOKIE: What you eating?

TERRY looks at the others. Stops chewing. DECCY struggles with him, takes the meat out of his hand.

DECCY: He's only gone and started on one of the monkeys.

TERRY: You what?

DECCY: That's fucking monkey you're eating there mate.

TERRY: It aint bad. Could do with a bit more salt.

COOKIE: (*Getting hysterical.*) You can't eat the monkeys. You can't. YOU CAN'T.

MAC: Alright Cooks…listen mate…you better stop.

TERRY: Fuck off.

MAC: I mean it. He don't like it.

TERRY: Look mate, either I eat this, or the way I see it, we got to start on each other. So who wants to go first?

TERRY eats. COOKIE stares at him.

You ever been down the Claydon then Mac?

COOKIE: No he never. But we been fostered aint we?

JEAN: That Mrs Galloway had me, she had that many kids. Give her two hundred quid a week for me – spent the whole lot down Lewisham on a Saturday and she never even give us no food. I told them, give me the fucking two hundred quid. Burnt her dog collection in the end, serve her fucking right.

COOKIE: Burnt her dogs?

JEAN: She had these toys. Stuffed fucking Alsatians, poodles…soaked them in lighter fuel and burnt the shit out of them. Had me arrested.

COOKIE: We can't be separated cause we're brothers – that's right isn't it Mac?

MAC looks at RORY.

MAC: Yeah, that's right.

TERRY: Saw your mum with that Billy Nailor yesterday. She's alright your mum.

MAC: What's that meant to mean?

TERRY looks at him.

What the fuck are you trying to say?

MAC squares up to TERRY. RORY stands up and looks out into the darkness.

RORY: There's a boat.

They all stand and look across the water.

(*Calling.*) Hello?

They look.

It's empty.

MAC: Think we can get it?

DECCY: That water's deep Mac.

RORY: I can get it. I'm a good swimmer.

MAC: It's cold man.

COOKIE: The water was up over the doorway in the barn…right up over it…our feet was getting wet.

RORY: The water's rising. We've got to move soon.

JEAN: We should get the boat.

RORY: I'll get it.

RORY starts to take off his shoes.

COOKIE: Don't go. We should all stay here. Stay together.

RORY: I'm a good swimmer Cookie. You take care of my chicken will you?

COOKIE: Don't go. She doesn't want you to go.

RORY: Give me that rope.

They tie a rope around RORY. He jumps into the water.

I'm under the bedclothes in Tom's bed. His plastic elephants are lined up under the sheet. It's Africa, and they're going for a drink at the waterhole…tramp tramp…tramp tramp…through the savannah…along the blue stripes of Tom's pyjama jacket…his arms are as thin as electric cable…tramp tramp…tramp tramp…the elephants climb up Tom's chest where the intravenous drip goes straight into the vein…when you're dead Tom can I have your bed…sure you can…but don't you pee in it…and when you're dead I'll come and find you…in heaven…how you gonna do that then…simple…I'll blow the silver whistle from the policeman's kit.

DECCY: I can't see nothing.

MAC: Ropes going out.

RORY: I come back from Margate…no Tom…no bed – no elephants. Must have chucked out all his toys. Didn't even let me go to the funeral. I never did find out what happened to that bed.

MAC: There he is!

COOKIE: He come back with the boat. Half full of water it was…

DECCY: You seen the state of it.

RORY: It isn't too bad…

DECCY: I can't swim mate.

RORY: We can bail it out.

DECCY: It aint big enough for more than two.

COOKIE: Water's come up to me feet Mac.

MAC looks around them.

DECCY: We get in that thing, we're all going to fucking drown.

MAC: We got to get in it.

DECCY: I'm not fucking doing it.

MAC: You got to. Two at a time.

TERRY stands up.

TERRY: Jeans first…and the baby.

DECCY: How'd you make that out?

TERRY: Stands to reason. She's got a baby.

DECCY: Why the fuck should you get the boat?

TERRY: What's it to you, you're the one saying you aint going to get in it.

TERRY starts to push JEAN towards the boat.

DECCY: You gonna let them do this Mac?

MAC: We got to go in twos.

DECCY: What if they don't come back?

Everyone looks at TERRY and JEAN.

What if they just leave us here to drown?

MAC: I'll go with her.

COOKIE: No Mac…I don't want you to go.

MAC: Be alright Cooks. There must be high ground somewhere near here. Drop off Jeanie and the baby…come back for you.

MAC makes his way towards the boat. TERRY pulls a machete out from under his coat.

TERRY: You aint getting in that boat.

DECCY: Where the fuck did you get that?

TERRY: Get in the boat Jeans…we're going.

MAC: What you gonna do, cut me head off?

TERRY: If I have to.

RORY: We can share the boat.

TERRY: Why don't you shut the fuck up. Get in the boat Jeans.

MAC makes a move towards TERRY.

I stabbed a boy down the Laurels once. I can do it again. Give us the DVD.

Reluctantly MAC hands down the box with the DVD.

MAC: You really think if we all rushed you we wouldn't be able to sort you out?

TERRY: Want to try? Come on then? Fuckers.

RORY: We don't want anyone getting hurt.

TERRY: Bet you fucking don't.

RORY: You slash someone with that thing Terry, you'll go to jail.

TERRY: Like I'm really bothered. Let's work that one out, go to jail, drown? Think I'll take my chances.

COOKIE: We aint drowning.

TERRY: Might be better off Cooks.

Everyone looks at TERRY.

Aint you told him then?

MAC and RORY stare at TERRY.

Secret. Oh I get it.

COOKIE: What's he saying Mac?

MAC: Take the boat. Come back for us.

TERRY: Hear that Jeans, they want us to have the boat now.

COOKIE: What's he mean Mac?

MAC: He don't mean nothing Cookie.

TERRY: Look good they do, your mum and that Billy Nailor. Getting married are they?

COOKIE: Mum and Billy Nailor?

TERRY: Won't want a kid that's mental will they?

MAC looks at TERRY, TERRY pulls the last of the knock off electrical goods into the boat. RORY steps forward.

COOKIE: I aint mental. Learning difficulties.

TERRY: Yeah right. Whatever. But they're going to put you away – I reckon they've your room booked down the Claydon right now – everyone knows – cause you're the kid that's always wanking in the park and Billy Nailor said down the Billiard Hall you should have been put away years ago cause you're old enough to be a pervert now, and there's no way he's going to marry your mum until she signs the papers. Ask Mac, he knows.

COOKIE stares at TERRY.

COOKIE: Water's that black now, black like the railings outside the Town Hall…

RORY: Black like the eye of an elephant making its way through the Savannah…

MAC: Black like marble headstones down the cemetery… as they…

RORY: Pull away –

MAC: Slowly…pushing with the oar…

DECCY: Fucking bastard! We'll fucking get you when we get back to the Laurels. We'll fucking kill ya!

TERRY: Fuck you wankers!

They all look from the roof of the shed.

JEAN: Rain's still falling….

TERRY: Never steered a boat before…

JEAN: Tes, what you look like?

TERRY: I dunno Jeanie but I reckon you're gonna tell me.

JEAN: Bloke on my Aunti's fucking biscuit tin.

TERRY: Oh yeah?

JEAN: Venice. Fucking gondola.

TERRY: Whatever.

JEAN: Know something?

Beat.

I love you Terry. I really do love you.

Back at the shed roof.

DECCY: You wanker. He wouldn't have cut you.

COOKIE: Mac?

DECCY: (*Shouting.*) We're coming after you, you shitfaced fucking scumbag.

COOKIE: Mac, what's he mean?

MAC: He don't mean nothing Cookie.

COOKIE: I aint going down the Claydon.

DECCY: The water is fucking coming up the roof man.

COOKIE: (*To RORY.*) My mum went to see you.

DECCY looks at RORY.

(*Realising.*) Fucks sake.

Beat.

Tonight, when you was with them black lads, you wasn't coming back was you?

MAC looks at him.

DECCY: You was going to leg it and leave me behind, that's why you had that bag. If those Peter's Street lads hadn't fucking grabbed us, you and him, you was going to be gone.

COOKIE: What's he saying Mac?

DECCY: You sold them some shit, how much did you get?

MAC: Fucks sake Deccy…

DECCY: (*Advancing.*) How much? Fucking tell me…

MAC: I'd have split it with you…

DECCY: Oh yeah, sent me some back in the post would you? You was legging it…

MAC: I aint got it no more have I? They took it off us…

DECCY: What you sell them black lads? FUCKING TELL ME!

MAC: Suger and shit.

DECCY: Fuck. Fuck.

MAC: We was going to be long gone.

DECCY: Not me. Not me! They'd have come after me.

MAC: No they'd never.

DECCY grabs MAC and pulls him to the ground. They struggle.

DECCY: You fucking lying bastard.

MAC: I needed the money Dec.

DECCY: I fucking need money. You would have fucking…

DECCY kicks MAC. Looks at him. Stands back.

I trusted you man.

MAC: I got to go Deccy. I needed the money so I could go.

COOKIE: I got money Deccy. I got two pounds, I hid it in my pants when they was kicking you.

DECCY: (*To MAC.*) You bastard. Fucks sake.

COOKIE: We got to go home now. I got to feed the fish.

MAC: You could have come too. I said, didn't I? New identities.

DECCY: Them black lads – they're bad man. I'll end up with both me legs broke.

MAC: So come with us.

COOKIE: Call mum on your mobile Mac.

MAC: Aint got my mobile Cooks.

COOKIE: (*With rising panic.*) Got to call Mum.

MAC: Aint got no phones have we?

DECCY: If we hadn't stopped to help that dead woman we'd have been well away by now.

COOKIE walks to the edge of the roof.

COOKIE: I'm going home now Mac.

COOKIE stands looking out across the water.

DECCY: Cooks that water's ten foot deep.

COOKIE: Got to go see mum now.

DECCY: Mac?

COOKIE: They can't put me in the Claydon can they Mac, cause, we can't be separated…

MAC: That's right Cooks…

COOKIE: I hate that Billy Nailor.

MAC: Fuck him.

COOKIE: Won't let mum tuck me into bed no more.

MAC: You got me to tuck you in, he can't stop me can he?

COOKIE: No one can stop you Mac.

MAC: Hey Cooks, you sure all them animals come up from down below. We don't want none of them drowning, do we?

COOKIE: Got them all Mac.

MAC: Best check anyway. Make certain. Deccy'll go with you.

COOKIE: Alright.

COOKIE moves away from the edge of the roof and heads for the hole with the ladder. MAC looks at DECCY, DECCY follows. RORY hands MAC a roll up. They both light up.

RORY: You read the casenotes then?

MAC: Left me in the office alone didn't you?

RORY: Maybe we can find him someplace better, special unit – something.

MAC: You got a brother?

RORY looks at him.

RORY: Yeah.

MAC: Put him in a special unit would you?

RORY looks at MAC, the words sinking in. They smoke.

RORY: Your mother – she's in a very difficult situation.

MAC smokes.

MAC: Yeah well, we're all in a difficult situation.

RORY: Where will you go?

MAC shrugs, smokes. DECCY and COOKIE climb back up with a sack each of monkeys.

COOKIE: We're going to set the monkeys free. The monkeys can't go to heaven if they aint had a funeral.

MAC: Monkeys don't have funerals Cooks.

COOKIE: They do. They DO. They gotta have a funeral.

MAC looks at him.

If we die, will we go to hell, for what we done?

MAC: What?

COOKIE: We done loads of bad things Mac.

MAC: We aint done no more than no one else.

COOKIE: I don't mind dying if I see Nan again.

DECCY: You think that Terry was right? That the war's come?

No one speaks.

We see the soldiers – Osama's fucking soldiers...we'll say...hey...mate...the names fucking Eddie Michaels and Demetreo Stavanos...

MAC: Fucking Greek aint we...

DECCY: Don't know nothing about these English bastards…

MAC: Aint never even lived here…wouldn't want to.

DECCY: And we'll just keep on walking.

The wind blows.

Scene Six

Morning. The water level has fallen. Debris is everywhere. Some of the barn has disintegrated.

COOKIE stands with his trousers rolled up, a dead monkey wrapped in sacking in his hands, and the rest in a sack at his feet.

COOKIE: When the water went down it looked dead weird, like everything was in the wrong place. All the plants and stuff was ripped up and stuck in between the branches of the trees.

MAC: (*Wading through.*) Hey Cookie…there's all sorts down here. Tools…fucks sake…there's a shoe.

COOKIE: They reckoned when the sea wall went, the water rolled on about fifteen miles before it stopped.

MAC: Oi! Dec! There's only a pair of fucking headphones.

MAC slips the headphones round his neck.

COOKIE: The polystyrene factory up Gravesend was pretty well tore up out of the ground…

RORY: (*His chicken under his arm.*) White stuff everywhere.

MAC: Killed the birds for a long time that did…

COOKIE: Poor birds.

RORY: Say more than a dozen people died that night…

MAC: Electricity cables killed a kid down Brighton…

DECCY: Fell in the fucking pram.

COOKIE: Water was full of dead things…even the worms drowned…

MAC pulls some dead worms off his trousers and chucks them away.

In the boat.

JEAN: Get a flat eh? Tes, one day, have a house maybe, with a garden, and a swing…

TES: Yeah. Why not?

JEAN: Kids should have a safe place to play.

TES: See that Jeans? Think I can see something. Yeah. Won't be long now.

JEAN: Take her to school in the car. Won't let no perverts get her. Keep her ever so safe, won't we?

COOKIE, RORY, MAC and DECCY stand in the water, facing us.

COOKIE: Give the monkeys a proper funeral…

RORY: Like they do in India Cookie, put them in the river…

COOKIE: Wrapped up every one…

MAC: Watched them drift away…

COOKIE: Mac said they'd go all the way to the sea.

MAC: Course they will Cooks.

COOKIE: Aint never seen the sea.

RORY: Thought about that woman in the offy, the one with the fluffy slippers…

MAC: Flood wasn't so bad back home...

DECCY: Not when you're twelve floors up a tower block on the Laurels anyhow...

RORY: Thought about her standing there, looking at me out through that grille, like something from San Quentin...

COOKIE: Got to sing a hymn now...

RORY: So we sang...

COOKIE: (*Sings.*) As o'er each continent and island...

MAC: (*Joining him...remembering.*) The dawn leads on another day...

RORY: The monkeys started to drift away...

DECCY: Hey Mac, you know where we'll go?

RORY: Thought about that poor boy up the Claydon, the one who cut himself...

DECCY: You gonna tell, about what happened here tonight?

RORY: Thought I saw Tom, for a minute...

COOKIE: You know where we're going Mac?

MAC: Course I do Cooks. Big city, biggest city we can find...

DECCY: You gonna tell on us?

RORY: No.

DECCY: And why the fuck should we trust you?

RORY: No reason.

Beat.

Wish I could come with you.

DECCY: No you don't.

COOKIE: You think they're in heaven now, those monkeys?

DECCY: Yeah Cooks. I reckon your Nan's just giving them all a nice cup of tea.

They all look out across the watery land.

COOKIE: (*Sings.*) Thy Kingdom stands and grows for ever Till all thy creatures own thy sway.

RORY, MAC, DECCY and COOKIE stand in the mud.

RORY holds the chicken.

The wind blows.

The End.